Best Easy Day Hikes
Yosemite National Park

Help Us Keep This Guide Up to Date

Every effort has been made by the author and editors to make this guide as accurate and useful as possible. However, many things can change after a guide is published—trails are rerouted, regulations change, facilities come under new management, etc.

We would love to hear from you concerning your experiences with this guide and how you feel it could be improved and kept up to date. While we may not be able to respond to all comments and suggestions, we'll take them to heart and we'll share them with the author. Please send your comments and suggestions to the following address:

Globe Pequot Press
Reader Response/Editorial Department
P.O. Box 480
Guilford, CT 06437

Or you may e-mail us at:

editorial@GlobePequot.com

Thanks for your input, and happy trails!

Best Easy Day Hikes Series

Best Easy Day Hikes
Yosemite National Park

Third Edition

Suzanne Swedo

FALCON GUIDES

GUILFORD, CONNECTICUT
HELENA, MONTANA

AN IMPRINT OF GLOBE PEQUOT PRESS

FALCONGUIDES®

Maps by Trailhead Graphics Inc. © Morris Book Publishing LLC
ISSN 1553-9903
ISBN 978-0-7627-5528-8

Printed in the United States of America
10 9 8 7 6 5 4 3 2 1

For Mom

Contents

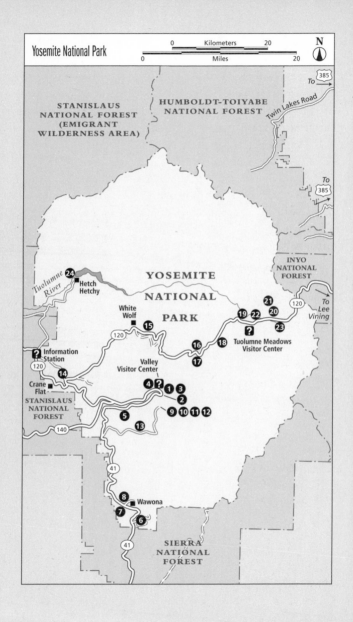

Kilometers

Miles

0

0

20

20

N

STANISLAUS
NATIONAL FOREST
(EMIGRANT
WILDERNESS AREA)

HUMBOLDT-TOIYABE
NATIONAL FOREST

Twin Lakes Road

To 385

To 385

INYO
NATIONAL
FOREST

Tuolumne River

24 Hetch Hetchy

YOSEMITE

NATIONAL

PARK

White Wolf

15

120

16

18

17

19 22 20

21

23

To Lee Vining

120

Tuolumne Meadows
Visitor Center

Information
Station

120

14

Valley
Visitor Center

Crane
Flat

STANISLAUS
NATIONAL
FOREST

140

5

4

1 3

2

9 10 11 12

13

41

8 Wawona

7

6

41

SIERRA
NATIONAL
FOREST

Acknowledgments

Thanks to the National Park Service, especially Ranger Mark Fincher, whose suggestions and advice were invaluable. Thanks also to the personnel and volunteers of the Yosemite Association.

Introduction

This book is for a great many of the nearly four million visitors to Yosemite National Park each year who have a limited amount of time to spend but want to sample some of the best features of the park on foot. Yosemite's borders encompass almost 1,200 square miles in east-central California, though the majority of tourists congregate in Yosemite Valley and miss much of the spectacular wild country beyond. The hikes described here are scattered throughout the entire park. All are accessible by paved roads, and none is difficult to find.

The hikes vary in length, but none is longer than 5 miles. The shorter hikes are not necessarily the easier ones. Because this is rugged country with few level places, most hikes do involve a little elevation gain and loss. Use the list of hikes ranked in order of difficulty to make your choice. All are on clearly marked, easy-to-follow trails.

Zero Impact

The trails that weave through Yosemite National Park are heavily used and take a real beating. Because of their proximity to pollution and dense population, we—as trail users and advocates—must be vigilant to make sure our passing leaves no lasting mark. If we all left our mark on the landscape, the parks and wildlands eventually would be destroyed.

These trails can accommodate plenty of human travel if everybody treats them with respect. Just a few thoughtless, badly mannered, or uninformed visitors can ruin them for

everyone who follows. The book *Leave No Trace* (www
.falcon.com) is a valuable resource for learning more about
these principles.

The Falcon Zero-Impact Principles

- Leave with everything you brought with you.
- Leave no sign of your visit.
- Leave the landscape as you found it.

Litter is the scourge of all trails. It is unsightly, polluting,
and potentially dangerous to wildlife. Pack out all your own
trash, including biodegradable items like orange peels. You
should also pack out garbage left trailside by other hikers.
Store a plastic bag in your pack to use for trash removal.

Don't approach or feed any wild creatures. The ground
squirrel eyeing your snack food is best able to survive if it
remains self-reliant—it is not likely to find cookies along the
trail when winter comes.

Never pick flowers or gather plants or insects. So many
people visit these trails that the cumulative effect of indi-
vidual impacts can be great.

Stay on established trails. Shortcutting and cutting
switchbacks promote erosion. Select durable surfaces, like
rocks, logs, or sandy areas, for resting spots. Be courteous
by not making loud noises while hiking.

Some of the trails described in this guide also are used
by horseback riders. Acquaint yourself with proper trail eti-
quette and be courteous. Consider volunteering time to trail
maintenance projects, giving something back to the parks
and trails you enjoy.

If possible, use outhouses at trailheads or along the trail.
Otherwise pack in a lightweight trowel to use to bury your
waste 6 to 8 inches deep. Pack out used toilet paper in a

plastic bag. Make sure you relieve yourself at least 300 feet away from any surface water or boggy spot and off any established trail.

Remember to abide by the golden rule of backcountry travel: If you pack it in, pack it out! Be sure to keep your impact to a minimum by taking only pictures and leaving only footprints.

Practice these principles of zero impact. Thousands of people coming behind you will be thankful for your courtesy and good sense.

Play It Safe

Generally hiking in Yosemite National Park is safe and fun. Though there are no guarantees, there is much you can do to help ensure each outing is a safe and enjoyable one. Below you'll find an abbreviated list of hiking dos and don'ts, but by no means should this list be considered comprehensive. You are strongly encouraged to verse yourself in the art of backcountry travel.

Know the basics of first aid, including how to treat bleeding, bites and stings, and fractures, strains, or sprains. Few of the hikes are so remote that help can't be reached within a short time, but you'd be wise to carry and know how to use simple supplies, such as over-the-counter pain relievers, bandages, and ointments. Pack a first-aid kit on each excursion.

The sun can be unrelenting in the Sierra Nevada; carry a sunscreen with a minimum 15 SPF and apply it often. The weather can change abruptly in any season. Carry clothing items to protect you from sudden and dramatic temperature changes and/or rain and snow. Remember, summer thunderstorms aren't uncommon in the mountains and may bring dangers such as lightning, hail, and high winds.

The mountains are home to a variety of wildlife, from squirrels to mountain lions. Squirrels can be hosts to disease, and mountain lions may attack if prompted by hunger. Rattlesnakes may be found on a few of these hikes, particularly from early spring to midfall. Watch where you put your hands and feet. If given a chance, most rattlesnakes will try to avoid a confrontation.

The same flora and fauna that make hiking such a relief from the daily grind also present potential hazards for unwary hikers. Know how to identify poison oak, which can be bothersome at lower elevations.

Ticks are another pest to be avoided. They hang in the brush waiting to drop on warm-blooded animals (people included). Check for ticks, and remove any before they have a chance to bite.

It is wise to bring more drinking water than you think you'll need. Generally bring thirty-two ounces for each hour of hiking per person. Most free-flowing water should be considered unsafe to drink if untreated.

You'll enjoy each of these hikes—whether short and easy or long and more challenging—much more if you wear good socks and appropriate footwear.

Carry a comfortable day pack containing snacks and/or lunch and extra clothing. Additional maps are not necessary for the hikes in this guide, but they are fun to have along. You also can pack other items to increase your enjoyment of the hike, such as a camera, a manual to help identify plants and wildflowers, and binoculars.

Bears

Yosemite's black bears pose little threat to hikers, but they do break into parked vehicles they suspect might contain food. Bears damage many cars each year. Bears' sense of smell is so acute they can detect a single wrapped and sealed candy bar in your trunk and may dismantle your car to get it. They are very intelligent; they know food comes in cans, ice chests, and paper and plastic bags, and they will break in to check out any of these items—even if they are empty.

Keep all ice chests and items that might appear to contain food hidden, and stow all food, fresh or freeze-dried, wrapped or unwrapped, in the bear-proof boxes provided at trailheads.

Shuttle Buses

Yosemite National Park operates free shuttle buses between trailheads and main points of interest. Between 7:00 a.m. and 10:00 p.m. during the summer season, the buses run every ten minutes in Yosemite Valley, every hour in Tuolumne Meadows, and every twenty minutes in the Wawona area. The *Yosemite Guide* newspaper, given to visitors at each park entrance, contains a map of bus routes and a schedule for buses in Yosemite Valley. You can pick up a Tuolumne Meadows schedule at the visitor center in Tuolumne Meadows.

The shuttles are a convenient, low-impact way to enjoy Yosemite. Trailhead parking is sometimes limited, and bears breaking into cars at trailheads is a concern. There is no gasoline available in Yosemite Valley.

Ranking the Hikes

The following list ranks the hikes in this book from easiest to most challenging.

Easiest
Most Challenging

Map Legend

═══(120)═══	State Highway
═══════	Local/Park Road
= = = = = =	Unpaved Road
▬▬▬▬▬▬	Featured Trail
- - - - - - -	Trail
～～～	River/Creek
—··—··—	Intermittent Creek
⬭	Body of Water
(⸱⸱⸱⸱)	Intermittent Lake
⸺⸺	Marsh/Swamp
⊔⊔⊔⊔⊔⊔⊔	Escarpment
▭	National Park/Forest
⏑	Bridge
▲	Camping
⫯	Gate
🖼	Nature Trail
P	Parking
▲	Peak
🏕	Picnic Area
▪	Point of Interest/Structure
♂	Spring
→	Trail Route Arrow
❶	Trailhead
🔷	Viewpoint/Overlook
❓	Visitor/Information Center
≋	Waterfall

Yosemite Valley

Yosemite Valley is one of the natural wonders of the world. Almost vertical walls rise up to 4,733 feet above the valley floor, where the Merced River winds its way through flower-filled meadows and shady forests. The famous profile of Half Dome dominates the east end and El Capitan the west. Some of the world's highest waterfalls pour from the cliffs. It is a mecca for hikers, climbers, photographers, fishermen, rafters, cyclists, and just plain tourists from every place on Earth.

While it covers only about 7 square miles of a national park that sprawls over 1,200 square miles, the majority of visitors stay in the valley. Indeed, many believe that Yosemite Valley and Yosemite National Park are one and the same. Do not expect a wilderness experience in Yosemite Valley, but don't assume that hiking there is not worthwhile just because it's popular. The valley's attractions draw so many sightseers because they are well worth seeing, but there are also many beautiful, quiet, out-of-the-way corners to enjoy on foot and in solitude.

The valley is open year-round and can be reached from the west via CA 41 from Fresno, CA 140 from Merced, and CA 120 from Manteca. In summer CA 120, the Tioga Road to the east and Big Oak Flat Road to the west, is open all the way through the park to the east side of the

Sierra near Lee Vining on US 395. A fee is charged per car for entering the park. *Note:* There is no gas available in Yosemite Valley.

Contact Yosemite National Park at (209) 372-0200 or visit the park's Web site (www.nps.gov/yose) for more information.

1 East Valley Floor

This flat hike, partly along the Merced River, passes through forests, meadows, and a swampy fen, with very fine views of North Dome and the Royal Arches. Along the way you can make an optional visit to the Happy Isles Nature Center and the site of a notorious rockslide.

Distance: 2.6-mile loop
Elevation change: Minimal
Approximate hiking time: 1 to 4 hours
Trail surface: Paved path, boardwalk, and forest floor

Difficulty: Easy
Map: *USGS Half Dome*
Best time to go: Year-round
Facilities: Food, supplies, phones, water, and restrooms at Curry Village

Finding the trailhead: Board the Yosemite Valley shuttle bus from anyplace in the valley and get off at Stop 13, Curry Village, or leave your car in the big parking lot at Curry Village at the southeast end of the valley. GPS: N37 44.16' / W119 34.16'

The Hike

From the raised patio area in front of the bustling Curry Village snack bar/grocery/bike rental complex, look beyond the enormous parking lot on your left (north) to towering North Dome and the Royal Arches, serene and indifferent to the hubbub below. Follow the paved footpath eastward past a line of tent cabins. About 100 yards beyond a driveway at the end of the tent cabin community, a second driveway turns right (south) into a parking lot for hikers and backpackers. Enter the lot, turn left, and walk to the southeast end. Take the unmarked but wide and obvious trail into the shady ponderosa pine and incense cedar forest.

Pass a little A-frame structure used for ranger/naturalist talks, and at 0.9 mile reach a swampy area known as The Fen. Here a boardwalk runs through a lush growth of water-loving horsetails, sedges, and fragrant mints. An interpretive panel explains what lives in soggy places like this one. The trail crosses a paved path at 1.0 mile just before meeting the Merced River. To the right (south) is the Happy Isles Nature Center, with wonderful exhibits and books inside. Behind the building you can see the rubble and smashed trees left by the 1996 rockslide that killed a hiker.

From the nature center backtrack to the north (downstream) and follow the riverside path to the shuttle bus road (Stop 16) at 1.1 miles. There are restrooms and a snack bar here.

This hike crosses the road and continues downstream along the north bank of the Merced, but take a minute to follow the road onto the Happy Isles Bridge for views of the river, which rushes toward the bridge in noisy whitewater rapids then emerges from the other side more quietly and sedately. The view of North Dome over the river on the downstream side is a photographer's favorite.

Once you have crossed the road, you leave the crowds behind and follow a path through incense cedars and pines, streamside alders, and dogwoods. Big, showy white azaleas perfume the air in May and June. The river changes character at every turn—sometimes gurgling busily, sometimes green and placid—occasionally splitting to flow around wooded islands. Horses and mules share this section of the trail, which connects the stables to the John Muir Trail.

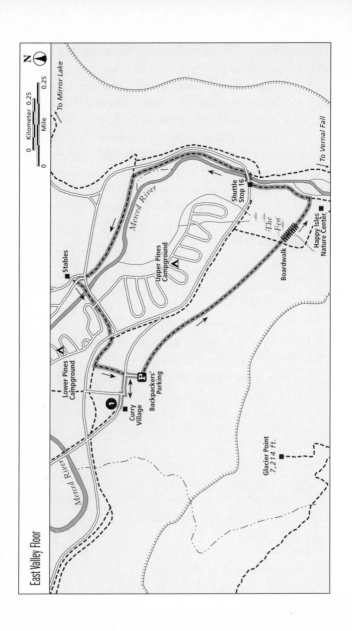

East Valley Floor

To Mirror Lake

Merced River

Stables

Lower Pines Campground

Upper Pines Campground

Curry Village

Backpackers' Parking

P

1

Merced River

Shuttle Stop 16

The Fen

Boardwalk

Happy Isles Nature Center

To Vernal Fall

Glacier Point 7,214 ft.

N

Kilometer 0.25

0

Mile 0.25

0

Remember to step off the trail to let them pass, since pack animals always have the right-of-way.

At 2.0 miles the stable area appears across the road on the right (north). Simultaneously Upper Yosemite Fall comes into view ahead. Turn left (west) and follow the road over the Clark Bridge, which spans the Merced. Pass between the entrances to Upper and Lower Pines Campgrounds. A sign directs you to Curry Village; just beyond you will spot the tent cabins for the village employees. The Curry Village parking lot and the end of the hike lie to the right (west).

Miles and Directions

0.0 Trailhead.
0.1 Reach the backpackers' parking lot.
0.9 Pass The Fen.
1.0 Reach the Happy Isles Nature Center.
1.1 Cross the Happy Isles Bridge on the shuttle bus road.
2.0 Pass the stables.
2.6 Return to Curry Village.

2 Happy Isles to Vernal Fall

This popular hike follows the first mile of the famous John Muir Trail along the roaring Merced River to where Vernal Fall plunges down the final step of the Giant Staircase. The way is steadily uphill, but the trail is short, mostly paved, and well worth the effort.

Distance: 1.6 miles out and back
Elevation gain: 400 feet
Approximate hiking time: 1 to 3 hours
Trail surface: Mostly asphalt
Difficulty: Easy

Map: USGS *Half Dome*
Best time to go: Spring through fall
Facilities: Snack bar, water, toilets, and phones at Happy Isles; water and toilets at the Vernal Fall Bridge

Finding the trailhead: Board the Yosemite Valley shuttle bus from anyplace in the valley and get off at Stop 16, Happy Isles. You can also park in the hikers parking area, marked TRAILHEAD PARKING, just east of Curry Village, though it is often full. There are bear-proof boxes where you can leave food and ice chests. GPS: N37 43.57' / W119 33.31'

The Hike

The Merced River first plunges over the steps of the Giant Staircase as Nevada Fall, then as Vernal Fall, before it slows to sweeping meanders over the flat floor of Yosemite Valley. If time permits, hike or drive up to Glacier Point for a spectacular overhead view of the Giant Staircase.

Happy Isles is the site of the notorious rockfall of July 1996. Cross the Happy Isles Bridge and turn right (south) at a sign indicating the Mist Trail, Vernal Fall, Nevada Fall, and the John Muir Trail. Follow along the east shore of the river for a few yards before heading into the forest. A short distance ahead, a huge sign marks the beginning of the John Muir Trail. The sign shows mileage to various points along the way to trail's end at Mount Whitney, 211 miles to the south.

The first part of this trail was recently repaved but is still a bit rough and rocky. Don't expect a true wilderness here. This is a popular spot for good reason: The view is spectacular. This trail is probably the most heavily used route out of the valley to the high country.

The trail climbs through black oak and pine forest among enormous lichen-draped boulders along the east bank of the Merced. A little spring trickles out of the rocks a few hundred yards up on your left. *(Caution:* Don't drink the water without purifying it.) The trail steepens gradually as you climb, but you will want to stop frequently to enjoy the roaring river through openings in the trees. After about 0.5 mile look across the Merced to your right (south). Tucked back up in Illilouette Gorge, the Illilouette Fall pours 370 feet down the Panorama Cliff to meet the Merced River. If you stop now and then to glance behind you, you will find that Upper Yosemite Falls is visible too.

The trail descends to the bridge at 0.8 mile, where dozens of visitors will be taking photos or staring in open-mouthed wonder at 317-foot Vernal Fall. There are restrooms nearby, a water fountain, and dozens of freeloading Steller's jays and ground squirrels. For their health and your safety, do not feed them. When you are ready, return the way you came.

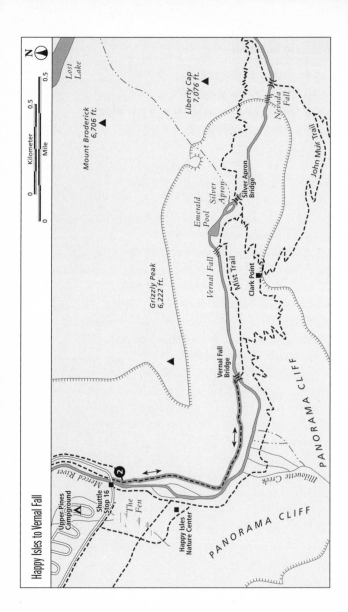

Happy Isles to Vernal Fall

N

0   0.5
Kilometer

0   0.5
Mile

Lost Lake

Mount Broderick
6,706 ft.

Liberty Cap
7,076 ft.

Grizzly Peak
6,222 ft.

Emerald Pool

Silver Apron

Nevada Fall

Silver Apron Bridge

John Muir Trail

Vernal Fall

Mist Trail

Clark Point

Merced River

Vernal Fall Bridge

Illilouette Creek

Upper Pines Campground

Shuttle Stop 16

The Fen

Happy Isles Nature Center

PANORAMA CLIFF

PANORAMA CLIFF

Miles and Directions

0.0 Happy Isles trailhead.

0.5 Views open to Illilouette Fall.

0.8 Reach Vernal Fall Bridge. Retrace your steps.

1.6 Return to Happy Isles.

3 Mirror Lake

The walk to Mirror Lake is a family favorite offering little beaches and shallow water to splash in during summer, classic reflection for photographers in spring, and always plenty of birds in the surrounding willows.

Distance: 2.0 miles out and back
Elevation change: 100 feet
Approximate hiking time: 1 to 3 hours
Trail surface: Part abandoned road, part forest floor
Difficulty: Easy
Map: *USGS Half Dome*

Best time to go: Year-round; best in May and June, when the dogwood's in bloom and the water level is high enough for Mount Watkins to cast the reflection that gives the lake its name
Facilities: Restrooms; no potable water

Finding the trailhead: Board the Yosemite Valley shuttle bus from anyplace in the valley and get off at Stop 17, Mirror Lake. The nearest parking lot with a shuttle bus stop is at Curry Village. GPS: N37 44.22' / W119 33.35'

The Hike

Mirror Lake was created when a rockslide dammed up a section of Tenaya Creek, which promptly went to work to reclaim its original course. Every spring it washes tons of silt down the canyon to refill the lake basin, extending fingers of earth into the water. This in turn invites colonization by water-loving plants like sedges and willows, which soon come alive with the songs of red-winged blackbirds.

Mirror Lake is well on its way to becoming Mirror Meadow. Eventually, as the basin fills in and dries out, the area may become forest with Tenaya Creek running through it, perhaps leaving the canyon as though Mirror Lake had never been—at least until the next major rockslide. A smaller, more recent rockfall occurred in March 2009 when Ahwiyah Point, the pointed projection just to the left (east) of Half Dome, dropped many tons of rock 1,800 feet, blocking the trail on the opposite side of Mirror Lake. The best view is from *your* side, however. Look for the fresh, light scars on the rock face.

For years the Park Service periodically dredged the lake, slowing the natural succession from lake to forest in order to preserve the popular reflection, but the practice was finally discontinued. Interpretive exhibits along the way help visitors appreciate the way the natural world continually transforms itself.

From the shuttle bus stop, the sign for Mirror Lake points you along the paved road (no longer in use except for bicycles), across the Tenaya Creek Bridge, and past an interpretive panel on the right (east) detailing the Yosemite flood of January 1997. That year, an unseasonable thaw sent runoff from a wetter-than-normal snowpack raging through the valley, gouging out the streambed and raising the water level to as much as 20 feet above normal. The flood washed out roads, bridges, campgrounds, and housing, temporarily closing the park. Beyond this panel you can leave the road and follow a signed footpath on the left (northwest) or continue on the road, which is the more scenic route since it follows the creek.

Both road and trail rise slightly, passing through a quiet forest of ponderosa pine, white fir, Douglas fir, incense cedar, and dogwood. At 1.0 mile the forest opens to reveal

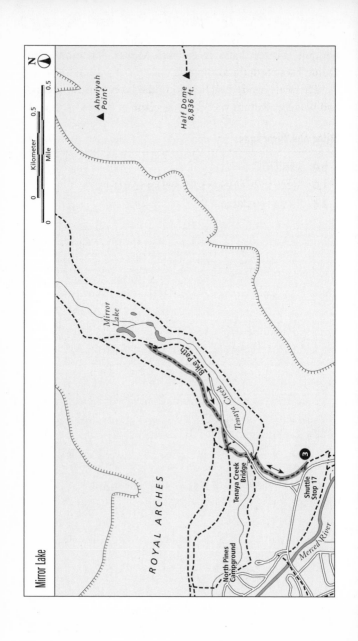

Mirror Lake

N

Kilometer
0   0.5
0   0.5
Mile

ROYAL ARCHES

Mirror Lake

Bike Path

Tenaya Creek

Ahwiyah Point ▲

Half Dome
8,836 ft. ▲

Tenaya Creek Bridge

North Pines Campground

Shuttle Stop 17

Merced River

❸

tranquil Mirror Lake, reflecting Mount Watkins. Half Dome rises abruptly to the east.

There are sandy beaches along the lakeshore for picnics and wading. Return the way you came.

Miles and Directions

0.0 Trailhead.

1.0 Reach shore of Mirror Lake. Retrace your steps.

2.0 Return to trailhead.

4 **Lower Yosemite Fall**

Yosemite Falls is among the most famous and frequently photographed falls in the world, and this walk gives you the closest top-to-bottom, head-on view you can get anywhere. The trail crosses a bridge so close to the base of the lowest fall that you can feel the spray early in the season.

Distance: 0.6-mile loop
Elevation change: Minimal
Approximate hiking time: 30 minutes to 1 hour
Trail surface: Asphalt, board-walk, and forest floor
Difficulty: Easy

Maps: *USGS Half Dome, Yosemite Falls*
Best time to go: Year-round; best Nov to mid-Aug. The falls are dry late summer and early fall.
Facilities: Pit toilets at the trailhead; food and supplies available at nearby Yosemite Lodge

Finding the trailhead: Ride the Yosemite Valley shuttle bus from any one of the 19 stops around the valley to Stop 7. GPS: N37 44.46' / W119 35.48'

The Hike

According to some, this is the highest waterfall (2,425 feet) on the continent. It is actually a series of three falls—the upper one dropping 1,430 feet, a middle series of cascades totaling 675 feet, and a lower one tumbling 320 feet—and qualifies as the highest only if all three are added together. In May and June the thunder of the water from melting snow falling onto the rocks below can be heard all over the valley, and the spray drenches onlookers hundreds of feet away. On full-moon nights in May, visitors may see the famous

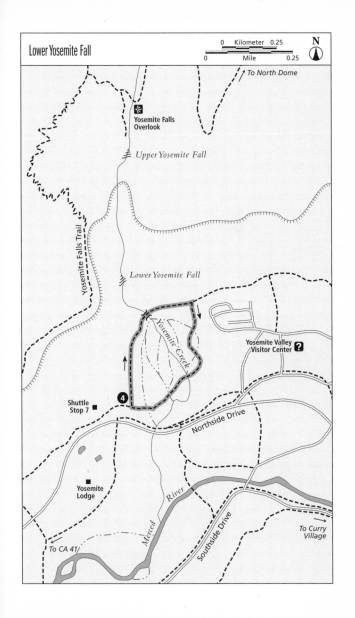

Lower Yosemite Fall

To North Dome

Yosemite Falls Overlook

Upper Yosemite Fall

Yosemite Falls Trail

Lower Yosemite Fall

Yosemite Creek

Yosemite Valley Visitor Center

Shuttle Stop 7

Northside Drive

Yosemite Lodge

Merced River

Southside Drive

To CA 41

To Curry Village

Kilometer

Mile

N

"moonbow" first described by John Muir. The volume decreases as the summer wears on, and by September the falls are usually completely dry. In winter the frozen spray forms an eerie ice cone at the base.

From the picnic area turn left. The newly reconstructed trail winds almost imperceptibly uphill through ponderosa pine and incense cedar forest toward the base of the falls to a wide viewing area and a bridge. At several points along the route are turnouts with interpretive panels about the human and natural history of the area that are well worth pausing to read. The bridge crosses the creek very near the base of the cliff. If it is early spring, you're sure to be dampened by the spray.

Despite posted warning signs, the huge slippery boulders are usually crawling with people. Beyond the bridge, the trail follows along the base of the cliff and then swings south behind some park employee housing. The trail winds past braided strands of the now-divided creek, curves again to parallel Northside Drive, and then returns to the starting point at the picnic area.

Miles and Directions

0.0 Trailhead.

0.2 Cross the bridge at Lower Yosemite Fall.

0.6 Return to trailhead.

5 Bridalveil Fall

Bridalveil Creek flows over the southern wall of Yosemite Valley through a defile between Cathedral Rocks and the Leaning Tower. But before it reaches the bottom, 620 feet below, the wind catches, tatters, and flings the droplets into graceful, lacy patterns. If you visit in springtime, you can expect to receive a shower from the spray.

Distance: 0.5 mile out and back
Elevation change: 50 feet
Approximate hiking time:
Trail surface: Asphalt
Difficulty: Easy

Map: USGS El Capitan
Best time to go: Spring through fall. The trail is icy and dangerous in winter.
Facilities: Pit toilets

Finding the trailhead: The parking lot is located on the Wawona Road (CA 41) about 1.5 miles after you emerge from the east portal of the Wawona Tunnel and before the road splits into Northside and Southside Drives, which are one-way roads. Watch carefully for the sign on the right (southeast). If you miss it, you'll have to drive all the way around the valley to get back. You cannot approach the waterfall by car from the east. Unfortunately the Yosemite Valley shuttle bus doesn't come this far. GPS: N37 48.00' / W119 39.04'

The Hike

Follow the trail signs up a wide paved path to a sign at a fork at 0.1 mile. Climb the right (south) fork along the tumbling boulder-strewn stream to the vista point near the base of the fall at 0.2 mile. In spring, when the fall is in full spate, you are bound to get soaked from the spray. The flow diminishes in summer and by autumn is often no more than

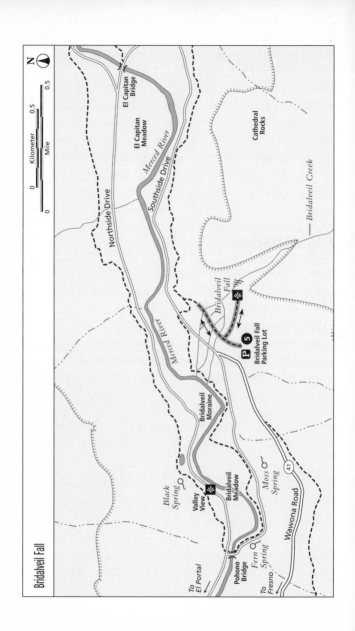

Bridalveil Fall

a trickle that disappears halfway down the cliff face. The wind shifts almost constantly, and the changing patterns of the falling water can be mesmerizing.

When you are ready, return to the trail junction at 0.3 mile. For a different perspective, turn right (north) at the fork and continue 0.1 mile, crossing three bridges over divided strands of the creek under an aromatic forest cover of bigleaf maple, bay tree, black oak, and incense cedar. Between the trees at 0.4 mile are framed views of the fall. Return to the parking lot the way you came.

Miles and Directions

0.0 Trailhead.

0.1 Reach a trail fork. Turn right.

0.2 Arrive at the vista point.

0.3 Return to the trail fork. Turn right (north).

0.4 Reach the lower viewpoint. Retrace your steps to the trailhead, passing the trail to the vista point on your left.

0.8 Return to the trailhead.

Wawona Area

The trails into the southern park begin from Wawona, Glacier Point Road, or the short spur road off CA 41 to the Mariposa Grove of Big Trees. Most trailheads start at around 4,000 feet and offer hiking opportunities earlier in the season than in other parts of Yosemite. You'll find more solitude in this part of the park too, because there is less water in high summer, the time when most people visit Yosemite.

Many of the southern trails begin near Wawona, about 4 miles inside the park from the CA 41 entrance and the site of a historic overnight stage stop on the way to Yosemite Valley. The beautiful old Wawona Hotel, built in the 1870s, is still in operation.

Just past "town," a new bridge crosses the Merced River; just past that is Chilnualna Fall Road on the right. The town has a gas station, gift shop, grocery store, and stables.

Call the office at (559) 877-2218 for more information.

6 Mariposa Grove

The giant sequoias are the largest living organisms on earth, and at up to 3,000 years old, they also are among the oldest. The bristlecone pines in the White Mountains to the east are older, and the coast redwoods are taller, but these are certainly the most massive and arguably the most awe-inspiring of the big trees. Yosemite has three groves of these trees. Mariposa Grove is the most popular, and the Grizzly Giant—your objective—is the largest tree in any of them.

Distance: 1.6 miles out and back (with optional loops)
Elevation change: 100 feet
Approximate hiking time: 1 to 2 hours
Trail surface: Mostly smooth forest floor
Difficulty: Easy
Maps: USGS Mariposa Grove; Mariposa Grove of Giant Sequoias Guide and Map by Jon Kinney, available at the trailhead for a small fee
Best time to go: Spring through fall, or until snow closes the road
Facilities: Restrooms, water, snacks, telephone, and a gift shop near the parking lot

Finding the trailhead: From the entrance station to Yosemite on the Wawona Road (CA 41) head right (east) for 2 miles to the Mariposa Grove. There is limited parking at the trailhead, but you can park in the lot across the street from the entrance station and ride the free shuttle bus. Or you can catch the bus in front of the store in Wawona. The buses run about every twenty minutes. A sign at the northeast end of the parking lot marks the trailhead. GPS: N37 30.06' / W119 36.40'

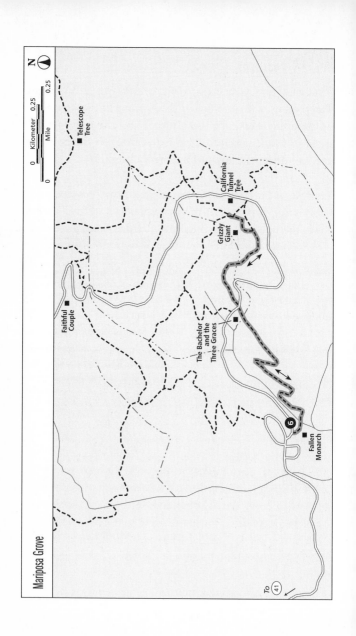

Mariposa Grove

Telescope Tree

California Tunnel Tree

Grizzly Giant

The Bachelor and the Three Graces

Faithful Couple

Fallen Monarch

6

To 41

N

0   Kilometer   0.25
0   Mile   0.25

The Hike

A narrated tram tour is available to those who prefer to ride. The tram uses the paved road that was built years ago, when private cars were still allowed inside the grove. A veritable maze of well-marked footpaths runs through the grove, so you can design a pleasant hike of any length.

The route described here takes you to two of the most famous trees in the grove. The trail is marked by a series of interpretive panels with fascinating tidbits of information about the trees, among them the fact that these giants have very shallow root systems and very tiny seeds and that they depend on fire to maintain their health and reproduction. In 2008 a small fire blackened a section of the grove near the beginning of the trail, creating an opportunity for you to observe how the forest regenerates itself over time.

From the busy parking lot, follow the signed trail (and the crowds) eastward along the main trail to the Fallen Monarch at 0.1 mile, made famous by an old photograph of a group of soldiers—on horseback—posed along the top. Cross the tram road and climb gently to a beautiful grouping called the Bachelor and the Three Graces at 0.3 mile.

The path climbs a bit more steeply for the next 0.5 mile to the massive beheaded Grizzly Giant at 0.8 mile. According to park literature, a single one of the nearly 3,000-year-old tree's lower limbs is larger than the trunk of any non-sequoia here. Other authorities maintain that it is larger than any other entire tree east of the Mississippi.

Just beyond the Grizzly Giant is the California Tunnel Tree. The tunnel was cut in 1895 for stagecoaches full of tourists to drive through. Years ago motorists could drive their cars through another of the sequoias here, the

Wawona Tunnel Tree, but eventually its roots weakened and the tree fell under the weight of an exceptionally heavy snowfall in 1969. From the California Tunnel Tree, return to the trailhead the way you came.

Miles and Directions

0.0   Mariposa Grove trailhead.

0.1   Reach the Fallen Monarch.

0.3   Pass the Bachelor and the Three Graces.

0.8   Arrive at the Grizzly Giant and, just beyond, the California Tunnel Tree. Retrace your steps.

1.6   Return to the trailhead.

7 Wawona Meadow

Wildflower lovers will find some rare and unusual species blooming along the trail in Wawona Meadow in early season. The shady path beneath a variety of conifers is a favorite stroll in summer, when the temperatures at this low elevation can be uncomfortably hot.

Distance: 3.5-mile loop
Elevation change: 100 feet
Approximate hiking time: 2 to 3 hours
Trail surface: Dirt road and smooth trail
Difficulty: Easy

Map: *USGS Wawona*
Best time to go: Year-round; Apr through June for wildflowers
Facilities: Lodging, store, gas, phones, and restrooms available at Wawona; pit toilets at the trailhead

Finding the trailhead: Drive to the little village of Wawona on the Wawona Road (CA 41). The Wawona Hotel is on the north side of the road, the golf course on the south. Just across from the hotel, a road cuts through the middle of the golf course. On the far side, the parking area and trailhead are marked by a big signboard with photos and information about the area. GPS: N37 32.11' / W119 39.23'

The Hike

You can follow the route in either direction, but it will be described counterclockwise here. The route follows an old, mostly dirt road that's no longer used by vehicles except at the spots where it crosses the Wawona Road.

Start by skirting the south side of the golf course under a cover of incense cedar and ponderosa pine. On the shady forest floor, watch for saprophytes—leafless plants that live

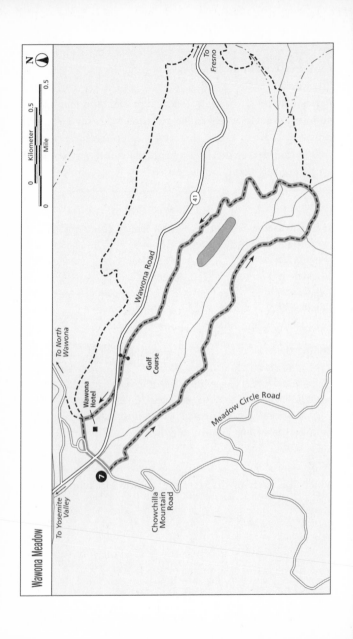

Wawona Meadow

N

Kilometer

Mile

0   0.5

To Fresno

41

Wawona Road

To North
Wawona

Wawona
Hotel

Golf
Course

Meadow Circle Road

7

Chowchilla
Mountain
Road

To Yosemite
Valley

on decaying material in the soil—such as the scarlet snow plant, the knobby brown spikes of pinedrops, and the odd little orchids called coral root. You can even find lady's slipper orchids in damp patches. In June great clumps of western azalea burst into bloom, along with several kinds of lilies.

The trail leaves the edge of the manicured lawn behind as the meadow begins. This border zone between forest and meadow, called the ecotone, is usually among the richest in living organisms. You might see a cluster of mule deer. They are very tame, but do not attempt to pet or feed them. Mule deer in Yosemite cause more serious injuries to tourists than do bears.

Now and then a little spur trail leads out into the meadow. There, down among the grasses and sedges, look for little three-petaled white star tulips in May. The tall cabbagelike stalks growing in clumps are the poisonous corn lily. There are islands of willow and chokecherry, usually broadcasting birdsong from warblers and blackbirds. It can be boggy and muddy toward the center and the vegetation is fragile, so step with care.

At 1.7 miles a trail alongside a little creek leads right (east) toward the park's south entrance. Continue along the road and step across another little rivulet. The road becomes partly eroded asphalt and runs through a section of forest in which the bases of the trees are slightly blackened from a management fire.

Cross the Wawona Road at 3.2 miles, just beyond the closed gate. The trail continues on to the Wawona Hotel where, at 3.4 miles, it crosses the road to the south and cuts back through the golf course to the trailhead.

Miles and Directions

0.0 Trailhead.

1.7 Cross the creek to the trail junction.

3.2 Reach the first crossing of Wawona Road.

3.4 Cross Wawona Road a second time.

3.5 Return to the trailhead.

8 Chilnualna Fall

Chilnualna Creek seldom flows quietly—it rushes and crashes and roars almost constantly for most of its length. One of the most spectacular sections of falling water is just above the point where Chilnualna Creek passes beneath Chilnualna Road and flows into the Merced River. It is as exciting as any of the more famous falls in Yosemite Valley, but few people see it, tucked away as it is in this little corner of the park. This trail takes you so close to the action that you're likely to get soaked from the spray if you go early in the year.

Distance: 0.4 mile out and back
Elevation change: 100 feet
Approximate hiking time: 30 minutes to 1 hour
Trail surface: Rocky forest floor, sometimes steep
Difficulty: Easy

Map: *USGS Wawona*
Best time to go: Spring through fall. The trail can be icy and dangerous in winter.
Facilities: Pit toilets and bear-proof boxes at the trailhead

Finding the trailhead: From the Wawona Road (CA 41) turn right (east) just beyond Wawona onto Chilnualna Road. Drive 2 miles, passing through the little village of North Wawona, to a signed parking area on the right. GPS: N37 32.53' / W119 38.05'

The Hike

Follow the trail signs from the parking area and cross the road to where a sign routes horse traffic to the left (north),

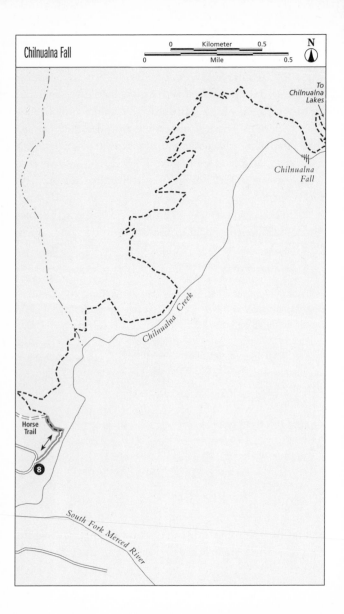

Chilnualna Fall

0 Kilometer 0.5
0 Mile 0.5

N

To
Chilnualna
Lakes

Chilnualna
Fall

Chilnualna Creek

Horse
Trail

8

South Fork Merced River

hikers to the right (east). The footpath heads steeply up, sometimes on big granite steps right beside the thundering water. The trailside mosses and ferns are green and lush from the fine spray. You go no more than 0.2 miles at creekside, but just standing next all that power is exhilarating.

Do not be tempted to continue scrambling up the slippery and treacherous rocks after the trail cuts left (to the west), away from the creek. Instead follow the trail to where it meets the horse trail that continues up into the high country.

You can return the way you came, but watch your step on the slick granite. If you prefer to make a loop, follow the horse trail back down along a paved road through a few little vacation homes to the parking area. This loop is 0.5 mile long.

Glacier Point Road

Many trails begin along Glacier Point Road, which cuts off from Wawona Road (CA 41) at Chinquapin, a junction about 14 miles from Yosemite Valley at 6,000 feet. The drive itself is beautiful, beginning among ponderosa and sugar pines, climbing through a red fir forest at almost 8,000 feet, then dropping to 7,200 feet at Glacier Point, 16 miles away.

Glacier Point is an extremely popular overlook 3,000 feet above the valley floor. It offers the best views of Half Dome, the valley, and indeed most of the park accessible by road. Almost all the hikes beginning from this road have spectacular views of the valley too. There is a snack bar, gift shop, phones, and toilets, along with an amphitheater for nighttime astronomy programs, and an area from which hang gliders are launched before 8:00 a.m.

The road is open all the way to Glacier Point spring through fall. Bears in the area mean you should not leave ice chests or food in your car. All trailheads have bear-proof boxes for food storage. A hiker's shuttle bus runs daily from the valley during summer. You can get a schedule and fares at the visitor center, or call (209) 372-1240. Reservations are required.

9 Glacier Point

The view from Glacier Point is surely one of the most spectacular in the world. Half Dome occupies center stage, brooding over slickrock Tenaya Canyon and Mirror Lake at the east end of Yosemite Valley. To the right the Merced River drops into the valley over the Giant Staircase as Nevada and Vernal Falls. Beyond lie rounded Mount Starr King and the darker colored Clark Range. Interpretive panels at the rim help you identify the distant peaks.

Distance: 0.5 mile out and back
Elevation change: Minimal
Approximate hiking time: 1 hour
Map: USGS *Half Dome*
Trail surface: Paved with some packed dirt
Difficulty: Easy

Best time to go: Spring through fall. Glacier Point Road is closed beyond the Badger Pass ski area in winter, but Glacier Point is a popular destination for experienced cross-country skiers.
Facilities: Food, water, telephones, restrooms

Finding the trailhead: From the Chinquapin junction on the Wawona Road (CA 41), drive up the Glacier Point Road about 16 miles to its end. You can also take a shuttle bus from Yosemite Valley to Glacier Point. GPS: N37 43.39' / W119 34.28'

The Hike

There will be no doubt about which way to go upon leaving the parking lot. Head toward Half Dome, which rears up out of the valley to the north and is backed by granite peaks that stretch to the horizon. About 200 feet past the restrooms, there's a big area map to the left (west) of the trail. To the right (southeast) is an amphitheater for nighttime astronomy programs and an area from which hang gliders are launched before 8:00 a.m. on summer mornings. You probably won't notice much of this, though, until you have absorbed some of the stupendous panorama.

Turn left along the path that passes below and in front of an old stone structure containing geologic exhibits about the formation of Yosemite Valley. Glacier Point itself lies slightly downhill and farther to the left (northwest). It is a narrow overhanging platform 7,214 feet above sea level that is bound to look familiar even if this is your first trip to Yosemite. Among the famous photos taken here is that of a group of old-time cancan dancers in midkick. Peer over the railing at Curry Village and the remarkably flat bottom of Yosemite Valley 3,000 feet below, where the Merced River snakes its way from one end to the other. The double waterfall across the way, above Yosemite Lodge, is 2,425-foot Yosemite Falls.

Until 1968 this was the site of the infamous "firefall." The bark of hundreds of magnificent old red firs from the nearby forest was set ablaze just after dark on summer evenings. After an elaborate ceremony of ritual calls between Glacier Point and the valley below, the glowing coals were raked over the cliff to form a fiery waterfall in the dark. It was a popular attraction, of course, but one more suited to an amusement park than to Yosemite. Lichens and other organisms inhabiting the rock face were seared away, and the beautiful old forest was threatened. The National Park Service ended the practice n 1968.

A park ranger is frequently on duty at Glacier Point to answer questions and give short lectures about the history and natural features of the area. Also on duty are innumer-

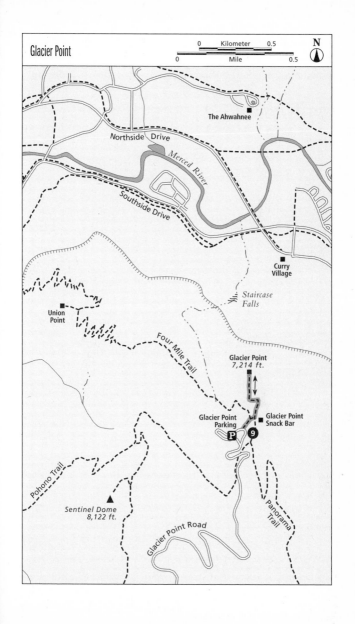

Glacier Point

0　Kilometer　0.5
0　Mile　0.5

N

The Ahwahnee

Northside Drive

Merced River

Southside Drive

Curry Village

Staircase Falls

Union Point

Four Mile Trail

Glacier Point
7,214 ft.

Glacier Point
Parking

Glacier Point
Snack Bar

P　9

Pohono Trail

Sentinel Dome
8,122 ft.

Glacier Point Road

Panorama Trail

able obese, panhandling California ground squirrels. Please do not feed them; this will only encourage their delinquency and endanger their health.

Miles and Directions

0.0 Trailhead.

0.3 Reach Glacier Point. Retrace your steps.

0.5 Return to the trailhead.

10 Illilouette Fall

This is an upside-down hike to the top of a seldom-seen waterfall and should probably be considered at the very upper limits of an easy day hike, but it isn't difficult if you take your time. Remember that it will take much longer to come back up from the fall than it did to go down. Make sure you have allowed plenty of time and that you carry water.

Distance: 4.2 miles out and back
Elevation change: 1,400 feet
Map: *USGS Half Dome*
Approximate hiking time: 3 to 5 hours
Trail surface: Packed earth and forest floor, sometimes rocky
Difficulty: More challenging

Best time to go: Spring and early summer. The trudge back uphill can be hot and dusty later in the season.
Facilities: Snack bar, gift shop, water, restrooms, telephones at Glacier Point; none at Illilouette Fall

Finding the trailhead: Follow the Glacier Point Road to its end 16 miles from Chinquapin on the Wawona Road (CA 41), or take the shuttle from Yosemite Valley to Glacier Point. From the parking lot walk straight toward Half Dome, which looms up out of Yosemite Valley to the northeast. Near the rim of the cliff turn right (east) onto the worn path and look uphill to find the big trailhead sign. GPS: N37 43.39' / W119 34.28'

The Hike

Before you begin, take a minute to enjoy the overwhelming immensity of the panorama at the trailhead. To the left is North Dome capping the graceful Royal Arches; in the center is Half Dome, the monumental symbol of Yosemite.

Tenaya Canyon stretches away to the northeast, and to the west runs the Merced River canyon, down whose Giant Staircase flow Nevada and Vernal Falls. Beautifully sculpted Mount Clark and the Clark Range stretch off to the east.

The only confusing section of the whole route is here at the beginning. Do not immediately strike out along the edge of the cliff to the left (north) of the trail sign. Instead head slightly uphill to the right (south). At 0.1 mile there are two more signs and two trails. To the right (west) is the Pohono Trail, which skirts Yosemite Valley to the west. The Panorama Trail, described here, goes left (south) toward Illilouette Fall.

The first 1.0 mile of the trail switchbacks downward through an area burned in 1987. Fragrant ceanothus and chinquapin, with its spiny green fruits, line the path. This is a good place to listen for the booming call of the blue grouse in spring and early summer. Males find a territory to their liking then sit and hoot, hour after hour, day after day, hoping to encourage a mate and discourage competitors. Their call is like the sound you make when you blow across the mouth of a glass bottle.

At 1.2 miles a trail coming from Mono Meadow to the south joins the Illilouette Fall Trail. Keep left (northeast) and continue to descend into the Illilouette Gorge. Shrubs give way to forest, and the rush of Illilouette Creek becomes audible. Other hikers have worn a little turnout to the left (north) of the trail to get a look at the fall, just out of sight of the trail itself. This is the only way to see most of Illilouette Fall from any direction because it is tucked so tightly back into the gorge.

Continue to descend a very few more switchbacks to reach the footbridge over the creek. The fall is not visible

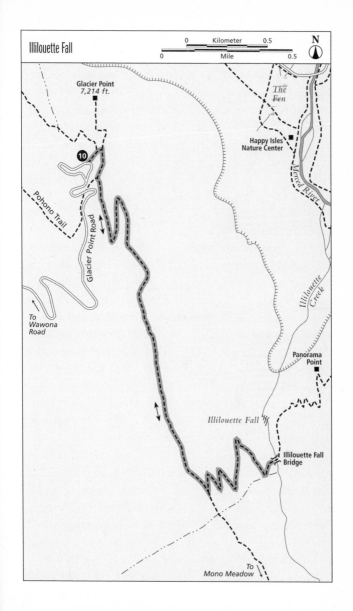

Illilouette Fall

0   Kilometer   0.5

0   Mile   0.5

N

Glacier Point
7,214 ft.

10

Pohono Trail

Glacier Point Road

To
Wawona
Road

The
Fen

Happy Isles
Nature Center

Merced River

Illilouette Creek

Panorama
Point

Illilouette Fall

Illilouette Fall
Bridge

To
Mono Meadow

from the footbridge, but the creek cascades down in picturesque wedding cake fashion. In springtime the blooms of
western azaleas lining the banks perfume the air.

Return the way you came.

Miles and Directions

0.0 Panorama/Pohono trailhead.

0.1 Reach the Panorama/Pohono Trail junction.

1.2 Pass the Mono Meadow Trail junction.

2.1 Reach the Illilouette Fall footbridge. Retrace your steps.

4.2 Return to Panorama/Pohono trailhead.

11 Sentinel Dome

The location of Sentinel Dome above Yosemite Valley provides complete 360-degree views of just about the whole park. Carry water and wear good sturdy shoes for this one; smooth-soled sandals won't give you enough traction on the smooth rock.

Distance: 2.2 miles out and back
Elevation change: 370 feet
Map: *USGS Half Dome*
Approximate hiking time: 1.5 to 3 hours
Trail surface: Forest floor and moderately steep slickrock

Difficulty: More challenging
Best time to go: Late spring through fall, whenever the Glacier Point Road is open
Facilities: Pit toilet at the trailhead but no water

Finding the trailhead: From the Wawona Road (CA 41) at Chinquapin, drive 13 miles east up the Glacier Point Road. Parking and the signed trailhead are on the left (northwest). GPS: N37 42.46' / W119 35.12'

The Hike

This dome, like the others in Yosemite, has its origin in the nature of the rock itself. Though the movement of glaciers did not produce it, the scouring action of ice did polish and smooth the rough edges.

Granitic rock forms when molten material under the Earth's crust rises toward the surface but cools and solidifies before it gets there. As the surface material is eroded, pressure on the underlying granite is decreased and the rock expands. The kind of granitic rock that forms Sentinel

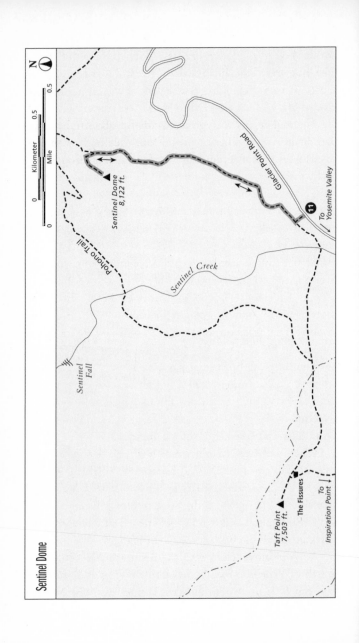

Sentinel Dome

N

Pohono Trail

Sentinel Dome
8,122 ft.

Glacier Point Road

To
Yosemite Valley

Sentinel Creek

Sentinel
Fall

Taft Point
7,503 ft.

The Fissures

To
Inspiration Point

Kilometer
0   0.5

Mile
0   0.5

Dome and others in Yosemite is so solid and massive that it does not break into pieces when it expands. Instead, great sheets of rock pop loose like layers of an onion and are eroded away.

The trail begins at a sign in a sandy opening in the forest that directs you to the right (northeast). The path to the left (west) goes to Taft Point and The Fissures. The rough and rocky path crosses a brook then undulates gradually upward, slowly revealing the top of the dome. Soon the trail curves to the left (north) and proceeds more steeply over smooth and featureless rock. Stenciled metal signs keep you on course.

At 0.4 mile a partly paved service road joins the trail from the right (east). Continue around the base of the dome on your left (west). When you have reached the "back," or more gradually sloping side, of the dome at 0.6 mile, the Pohono Trail splits off to the right (north) and heads down to Glacier Point. Turn left (west) just past this point, and head up the steep open slope on an indistinct "path." Don't worry if you lose the track—the only way to go is up. At the dome's summit are the remains of a gnarled Jeffrey pine, once the subject of innumerable photographs and postcards. Dead now and fallen, it is still picturesque.

When you have caught your breath, make a slow circle around the summit. To the northwest, Yosemite Valley, flanked by the Cathedral Rocks on the left (south) and El Capitan on the right (north), stretches toward the coast. If the Great Central Valley is free of smog (a rare occurrence), you can see all the way to the Coast Ranges.

As you move clockwise to the northeast, the entire length of Yosemite Falls comes into view. In early summer you can hear its roar from here. Farther east, the Merced

River canyon and Nevada Fall appear and then Mount Clark and the colorful Clark Range, providing a spiky backdrop for the rounded tops of Mount Starr King. The circle is closed by the lower forested country to the south.

When you are ready, return the way you came. Descend very slowly and carefully, avoiding loose sand and gravel whenever possible and taking care to follow the metal signs directing you to the parking lot.

Miles and Directions

0.0 Trailhead.

0.4 Reach the service road.

0.6 Pass the Pohono Trail to Glacier Point.

1.1 Reach the top of Sentinel Dome. Retrace your steps.

2.2 Return to the trailhead.

12 Taft Point and The Fissures

This is an upside-down excursion. After an easy cruise downhill to Taft Point, you will be climbing up on your way back. Be sure to give yourself plenty of time, and take water with you. Your reward is a striking set of geologic features that will help you understand how Yosemite got its famous profile, with a magnificent—and spine-tingling—view of Yosemite Valley as a bonus.

Distance: 2.2 miles out and back
Elevation change: 250 feet
Map: *USGS Half Dome*
Approximate hiking time: 2 to 3 hours
Trail surface: Forest floor and slickrock
Difficulty: Moderate

Best time to go: Spring through fall, when the Glacier Point Road is open
Facilities: Pit toilet at the trailhead but no water; snacks and telephones available at Glacier Point, another 3 miles down the road

Finding the trailhead: From Chinquapin on the Wawona Road (CA 41), turn east onto the Glacier Point Road. Drive 13 miles to the parking area and signed trailhead, which are on the on the left (west). GPS: N37 42.46' / W119 35.12'

The Hike

The trail begins at a sign in a sandy opening in the mixed pine and fir forest. Follow the path to the left (west) fork. Sentinel Dome lies to the right (north). Pass through a flat, fairly open stretch past an odd, isolated outcrop of almost pure-white quartz on the right, then swing left (south) and start downhill where the forest closes in. At 0.4 mile reach

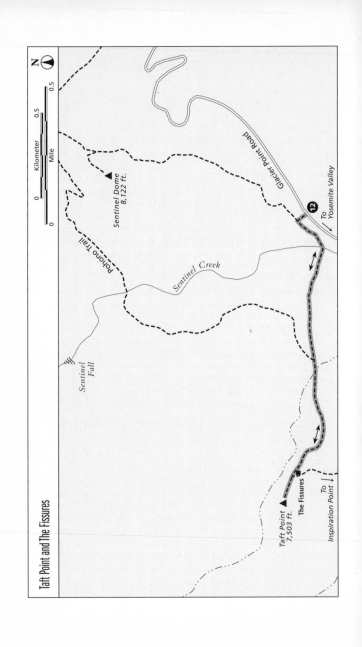

Taft Point and The Fissures

N

0   Kilometer   0.5

0   Mile   0.5

Pohono Trail

Sentinel Dome
8,122 ft.

Sentinel Creek

Sentinel
Fall

Glacier Point Road

12

To
Yosemite Valley

Taft Point
7,503 ft.

The Fissures

To
Inspiration Point

the Pohono Trail junction; continue walking left (west). The trail sign here says you have come only 0.2 mile from the trailhead, but this mileage is out of date.

The forest deepens, and a little creek you will soon cross nourishes a colorful garden of moisture-loving cow parsnip, senecio, corn lily, knotweed, and shooting star. The trail emerges from the shady forest onto open rock and becomes steeper. The flower-filled gully on your right (north) abruptly narrows, deepens, and drops through a notch that sends its little creek plummeting toward the valley floor.

Descend carefully down the rocks past low patches of manzanita and the occasional Jeffrey pine. When the terrain begins to level out, watch for The Fissures on the right. These narrow, deep cracks, or joints, in the granite—up to 40 feet long and slicing inward from the edge of the over-hanging cliff—are not visible until you are standing right at their edges. Peering carefully down into one of these cracks, you can see that they cut completely through yards and yards of solid granite, below which there is nothing but about 3,000 feet of thin air between you and the floor of Yosemite Valley. Because of the exposure, this is not a good choice for an evening hike in low light or for a walk with small, unrestrained children.

Once your internal butterflies have settled, proceed toward a slightly rising point with a protective iron railing around it that leans out over the valley like the prow of a ship. This is Taft Point (1.1 miles). Directly across are the Three Brothers, produced by the same jointing process that opened the rock fissures. To the left (west) is the vertical face of El Capitan; to the right (east) is Yosemite Falls. If you stroll westward along the rim, you can see the dramatic knife edges and needlelike spikes of Cathedral Spires.

When you are ready to return, descend the rise from Taft point to the first trail sign. (There is a second sign beyond this one. Don't go that far.) The right-hand fork heads south along the Pohono Trail to Inspiration Point. The left southeast) fork returns to the trailhead and parking area.

Miles and Directions

0.0 Trailhead.

0.4 Reach the Pohono Trail junction.

0.9 Pause at The Fissures.

1.1 Arrive at Taft Point. Retrace your steps.

2.2 Return to the trailhead.

13 McGurk Meadow

This is one of Yosemite's prettiest and "bloomingest" meadows. Most visitors drive right past the unobtrusive trailhead to this little slice of paradise on their way to Glacier Point, so you might be lucky enough to have it all to yourself.

Distance: 1.6 miles out and back
Elevation change: Negligible
Approximate hiking time: 1 to 2 hours
Trail surface: Forest floor and slushy meadow

Difficulty: Easy
Maps: USGS *El Capitan* and *Half Dome*
Best time to go: All summer; wildflowers best in July
Facilities: None at the trailhead

Finding the trailhead: Drive about 8.5 miles up the Glacier Point Road from the junction with Wawona Road (CA 41) at Chinquapin. The trailhead is just before the entrance to Bridalveil Creek Campground, but it's easy to miss. The campground is on the right (south) side of the road; the trailhead is on the left (north). The easiest way to find the trailhead is to drive to the campground entrance, turn around, and head back (west) the way you came for about 200 yards. Park in the first turnout on the right. The trailhead sign is about 100 yards ahead, but there is nowhere to park near the sign. GPS: N37 40.14' / W119 37.41'

The Hike

The path to the meadow descends through quiet lodgepole pine forest. Currants, strawberries, lupines, larkspur, and many other species flourish alongside the trail.

Just before you reach the meadow at 0.7 mile, watch for an old log cabin on the left (west). Beyond, at 0.8 mile, lies

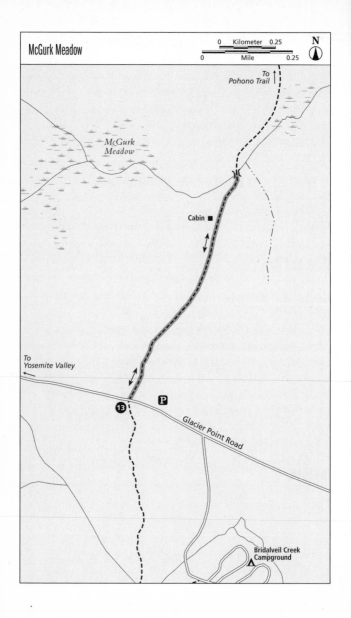

McGurk Meadow

McGurk
Meadow

To
Pohono Trail

Cabin ■

To
Yosemite Valley

13

P

Glacier Point Road

Bridalveil Creek
Campground

N

0   Kilometer   0.25

0   Mile   0.25

the meadow. It is threaded by a little brook and spangled with wildflowers of every color: shooting star, lungwort, corn lily, monkeyflower, and paintbrush, to name a few. The meadow is a fairly long one. The flower gardens continue for almost 2 miles, beyond which the McGurk Meadow Trail meets the Pohono Trail.

If you don't care to venture so far into the meadow, you can find a pleasant spot near the footbridge to linger along its edges. Such a meeting of forest and meadow is one of the best places for wildlife watching during the morning and evening hours.

Retrace your steps to the trailhead.

Miles and Directions

0.0   Trailhead.

0.7   Pass the old log cabin.

0.8   Reach McGurk Meadow. Retrace your steps.

1.6   Return to the trailhead.

Tioga Road

The Tioga Road (CA 120) is the only automobile route that runs all the way across Yosemite. Hikes on this side of the valley start later in the year than those on the south because the snow lasts longer in the shady hollows and valleys. Many of the streams are too fast, too wide, and too deep to cross safely until well into July.

All the hikes in this section are reached from the Tioga Road. There are high peaks, passes, waterfalls, and sensationally beautiful scenery; but overall the terrain is slightly less rugged and the average elevation is a little lower than the country to the south. Furthermore, there are no trails heading directly into Yosemite Valley. The nearest source of supplies—and it's minimal—is the gas station at Crane Flat, at the east end of the road. Tuolumne Meadows, the only developed area, has a visitor center, store, cafe, mountaineering shop, campground, lodge, and gas station.

A free shuttle bus runs between Tuolumne Lodge and Olmsted Point every hour. The Tuolumne Meadows hikers' bus leaves Yosemite Valley and stops at Crane Flat and White Wolf on the way to Tuolumne Meadows Lodge every day. There is a charge, the amount depending upon where you want to be dropped off. A schedule and map of shuttle stops are available at the visitor center.

14 Tuolumne Grove

The Tuolumne Grove of giant sequoias is not as heavily visited as the Mariposa Grove. And because it does not have a tram tour through it, you can enjoy the beauty and serenity of the forest away from the sounds of "civilization."

Distance: 2.0-mile lollipop
Elevation change: 480 feet
Approximate hiking time: 1 to 2 hours
Trail surface: Abandoned road
Difficulty: Moderate

Map: *USGS Ackerson Mountain*
Best time to go: Spring through fall, whenever the road is open
Facilities: Toilets but no water at the parking lot

Finding the trailhead: From Yosemite Valley drive 16 miles north on the Big Oak Flat Road (CA 120) to Crane Flat. Turn right (east) onto the Tioga Road (a continuation of Highway 120) and drive less than 1 mile to the Tuolumne Grove parking area on the left (west). GPS: N37 45.28' / W119 48.17'

The Hike

The route follows an old road now closed to vehicle traffic. It passes through a closed gate and descends in a beautiful old forest of white fir, Douglas fir, sugar pine, and incense cedar. This last, with its smooth red bark, is often confused with the giant sequoia, but the first of those will not appear for about 0.5 mile. In spring, exquisite white dogwoods bloom in openings in the forest.

The first huge sequoia with an interpretive panel beside it appears on the left (west) at about 1.0 mile. A sign to the right (north) directs you to the Tunnel Tree. This tree was

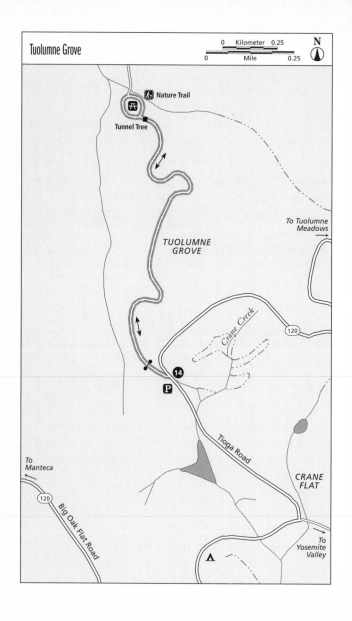

already just a stump when the tunnel was cut through it in 1878, but dead or alive, it evokes an eerie feeling when you look straight up from the inside.

Beyond the Tunnel Tree is a picnic area that used to be a parking lot when cars were allowed through the grove. The Nature trail begins here on the right (northeast) across a little bridge. The trail has a series of excellent interpretive signs explaining the natural history of the trees: how they reach their great ages of up to 3,000 years; how they are adapted to survive repeated fires; how they depend on fires, insects, and squirrels to reproduce; and more. The nature trail loop returns to the road at the picnic area. Climb back up the road to the trailhead.

Miles and Directions

0.0 Trailhead.

1.0 Reach Tuolumne Grove and the nature trail loop.

2.0 Return to the trailhead.

15 May Lake

May Lake High Sierra Camp is one of five popular back-country camps with tent cabins and other amenities that are available to visitors by reservation only. You can hike in to spend the day with little effort, since it is the nearest of all the camps to a road (not counting Tuolumne Meadows Lodge). Mount Hoffman, at the geographical center of Yosemite, provides the backdrop to this idyllic lake.

Distance: 2.4 miles out and back
Elevation change: 500 feet
Approximate hiking time: 2 to 4 hours
Trail surface: Rocky forest floor and switchbacks
Difficulty: Moderate
Map: *USGS Tenaya Lake*
Best time to go: All summer, whenever the Tioga Road is open and free of snow
Facilities: No trailhead facilities; toilets and water at May Lake. Please use the toilets at the campground, not at the High Sierra Camp. A small store at the High Sierra Camp is open for a few hours each day.

Finding the trailhead: The May Lake Road junction lies along the Tioga Road (CA 120) 27 miles east of Crane Flat and 20 miles west of Tioga Pass. Follow the narrow road north about 2 miles to the trailhead. Drive with care. In many places the road is only wide enough for one vehicle at a time. Leave any food or ice chests in the bear-proof boxes at the trailhead. GPS: N37 49.57' / W119 29.28'

The Hike

The hike begins in a shady glen with a variety of conifers—lodgepole, silver pine, hemlock, and fir—and passes a little brown pond teeming with fairy shrimp and other interesting

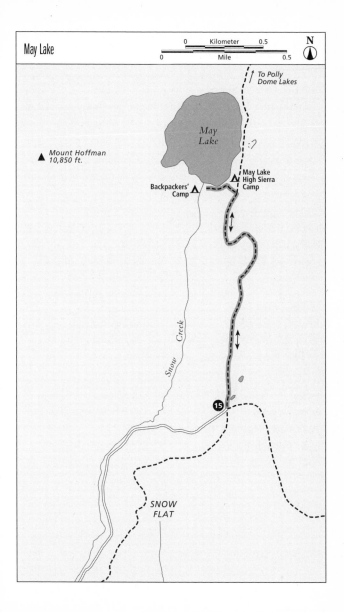

May Lake

Kilometer
0   0.5

Mile
0   0.5

N

To Polly
Dome Lakes

May
Lake

Mount Hoffman
10,850 ft.

May Lake
High Sierra
Camp

Backpackers'
Camp

Snow Creek

15

SNOW
FLAT

creatures. The well-used trail climbs slowly at first, passing through granite corridors where cracks bloom with ferns, mountain's pride penstemon, shaggy hawkweed, and other wildflowers.

The trail ascends gradually then begins a steeper, winding climb. There are good views now and then down Tenaya Canyon past Clouds Rest and Half Dome. The dramatic pointy peak in the distance is Mount Clark. Back up the canyon to the right (southeast), you can just glimpse Tenaya Lake.

The trail flattens out in forest and in just a few yards reaches a trail fork at May Lake at 1.2 miles. To the left (west) is the camping area; to the right (east) is the High Sierra Camp, marked by a row of white tent cabins. There is a backpacker campground nearby.

Enjoy the lakeshore, but do not jump in. This is the local water supply, and swimming is prohibited. Mount Hoffman (10,850 feet) rises dramatically behind the lake to the west.

Miles and Directions

0.0 Trailhead.
1.2 Reach May Lake. Retrace your steps.
2.4 Return to the trailhead.

16 Olmsted Point Nature Trail

Most visitors hop out of their cars here, take a snapshot of the view, and then drive away. By descending only a very short distance from the parking lot, however, you enter a different world where you can feel the wind in the rocks and hear the chuckling of grouse and the whistle of marmots.

Distance: 0.6 mile out and back
Elevation change: 300 feet
Approximate hiking time: 30 minutes to 1 hour
Trail surface: Granite
Difficulty: Easy

Map: *USGS Tenaya Lake*
Best time to go: All summer, whenever the Tioga Road is open and trails are free of ice
Facilities: None at the trailhead

Finding the trailhead: Drive about 9 miles west of the Tuolumne Meadows Visitor Center on the Tioga Road (CA 120). Watch for the signed parking area on the south side of the road a little more than 1 mile southwest of Tenaya Lake. GPS: N37 48.42' / W119 29.01'

The Hike

Begin at the interpretive panel about the formation of Yosemite's domes to find the stupendous gorge of Tenaya Canyon yawning all around you. To the south, the exfoliating granite of Clouds Rest forms intricate patterns. Half Dome lies beyond. Behind you to the north is Tenaya Lake—deep, deep blue in its basin of ice-polished granite.

Proceed downhill along a rock-lined path to a trail junction. The right (west) fork goes down to Yosemite Valley; the left (northeast) fork skirts the Tioga Road heading to

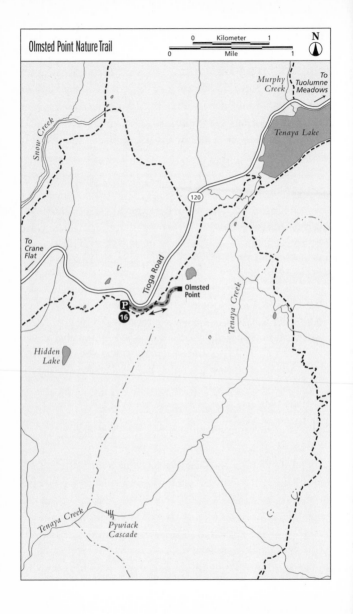

Kilometer

Mile

N

Snow Creek

Murphy Creek

To Tuolumne Meadows

Tenaya Lake

120

To Crane Flat

Tioga Road

Olmsted Point

P
16

Tenaya Creek

Hidden Lake

Tenaya Creek

Pywiack Cascade

Tenaya Lake. Follow the trail straight ahead, marked with the sign that says NATURE TRAIL, and climb a winding path lined with magenta mountain's pride penstemon and pink spirea to the top of a rocky rise. This is the best spot in Yosemite to learn how to identify Sierra trees. In this one small area an amazing number of conifer species are jumbled together: junipers; white firs; and lodgepole, Jeffrey, white-bark, and western white pines.

Watch your step as you first descend, then ascend the slope to the trail's end at 0.3 mile. The fine sand covering the smooth rock can be slippery. Please do not feed the squirrels and marmots. They need to forage for the proper food to get them through their long winter hibernation.

Miles and Directions

0.0 Trailhead.

0.3 Arrive at trail's end. Retrace your steps.

0.6 Return to the trailhead.

17 Tenaya Lake

Tenaya Lake was named for Chief Tenaya who, with all his people, was driven from his home in Yosemite by the U.S. Cavalry. It is a very big lake by Yosemite standards—a very popular one too, with its wide sandy beach and proximity to the road. This hike takes you around the "back" side of the lake, away from the busy highway.

Distance: 3.0 miles out and back
Elevation change: Negligible
Approximate hiking time: 1 to 3 hours
Trail surface: Forest floor

Difficulty: Easy
Map: *USGS Tenaya Lake*
Best time to go: All summer, whenever the Tioga Road is open
Facilities: Toilets and bear-proof boxes at the trailhead

Finding the trailhead: Ride the free shuttle bus from Tuolumne Meadows to Stop 9 at the northeast end of Tenaya Lake, or drive to the same spot on the Tioga Road (CA 120). Turn southeast into the picnic area parking lot, where you will find toilets, bear boxes, and a sign directing you to the trail. There is another picnic area about half-way along the length of the lake just off the Tioga Road, but the trail begins at the picnic area at the northeast end of the lake. GPS: N37 50.16' / W119 27.08'

The Hike

Follow the trail sign to the picnic tables on the beach, and head south along the shore. Unless it is quite late in summer, you will probably have to wade the inlet creek at 0.2 mile. The beach is a good vantage point from which to watch climbers clinging to the bare rock faces of the surrounding domes.

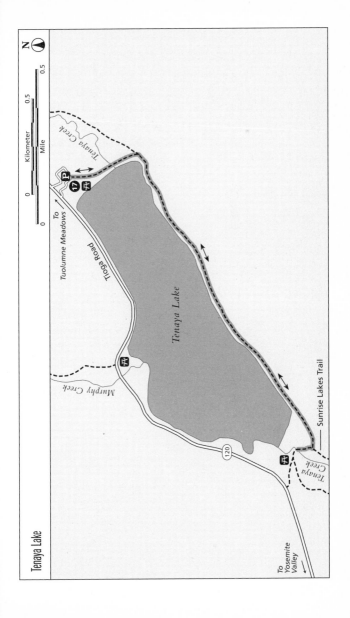

Tenaya Lake

Pick up the obvious trail that runs alongside the lake's south shore. Stroll through garden after garden of wildflowers beside several trickling brooks. Wander as far as you wish along the lakeside before returning to the trailhead.

You can circumnavigate the entire lake, but once you reach its north side, you must walk on the shoulder of busy Tioga Road for the whole length of the lake to get back to the parking lot.

Miles and Directions

- **0.0** Trailhead.
- **0.2** Cross the inlet creek.
- **1.5** Reach the Sunrise Lakes Trail. Retrace your steps.
- **3.0** Return to the trailhead.

Option:

Continue an additional 1.5 miles to the Sunrise Lakes trailhead. Turn right (west) and follow the trail to Tioga Road. Pick up the shuttle at Stop 10 and ride it back to Stop 9.

18 Lukens Lake

This easy and popular hike through forest and meadow to a quiet lake is a favorite with wildflower lovers.

Distance: 1.6 miles out and back
Elevation change: 150 feet
Approximate hiking time: 1 to 2 hours
Trail surface: Forest floor and slushy meadow

Difficulty: Easy
Map: *USGS Yosemite Falls*
Best time to go: All summer, whenever the Tioga Road is open; wildflowers best in July
Facilities: None at the trailhead

Finding the trailhead: Drive on the Tioga Road (CA 120) about 2 miles east of the White Wolf junction. The signed parking area is on the south side of the road; the trail begins on the north side. GPS: N37 51.04' / W119 36.53'

The Hike

To begin this hike, carefully cross the Tioga Road and head uphill through an almost pure red fir forest. The cones underfoot come from the occasional western white pine or hemlock. Fir cones do not fall—they decompose and release their seeds while still on the tree. Watch for odd, leafless plants like pinedrops, brilliant red snow plant, and little coral root orchids on the forest floor. Because these species have no green leaves and thus cannot make food for themselves through photosynthesis, they live on decaying material in the soil. Chinquapin—green-and-gold shrubs with spiny but delicious edible nuts—grow in the sunny spots.

The trail tops a rise and then descends to a creek filled with dozens of species of waist-high wildflowers. This dis-

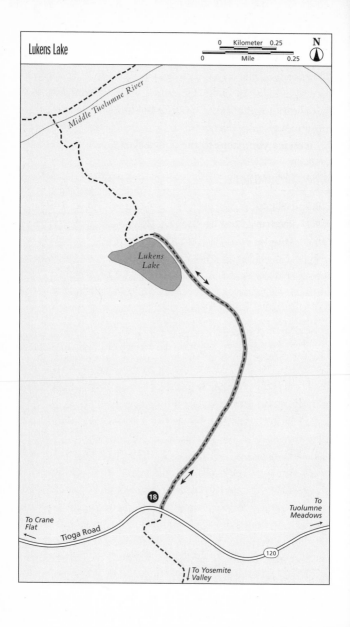

Lukens Lake

Middle Tuolumne River

Lukens
Lake

18

To Crane
Flat

Tioga Road

To
Tuolumne
Meadows

120

To Yosemite
Valley

play makes Lukens Lake a favorite with wildflower lovers. The trail turns left (northwest) and follows the creek to Lukens Lake. The lake is shallow, grassy, and muddy around the edges—not the best choice for a swim. The moisture that allows for the lushness of the wildflowers means lots of mosquitoes. Take repellent.

Retrace your steps to the Tioga Road.

Miles and Directions

0.0 Trailhead.

0.7 Reach and follow the creek.

0.8 Arrive at Lukens Lake. Retrace your steps.

1.6 Return to the trailhead.

Tuolumne Meadows

The Grand Canyon of the Tuolumne River dominates this region and defines its northern boundary. The Lyell Fork of the Tuolumne originates at the Lyell Glacier, and the Dana Fork rises from the snowfields of Mount Dana, both to the south. The forks meet in Tuolumne Meadows and wander languorously northwest for a few miles before beginning their headlong rush toward the Pacific Ocean in an almost continuous series of cascades and waterfalls. The canyon they have carved was gouged even deeper by glaciers, which produced a narrow slot in the granite with vertical walls that are in some places higher than those of Yosemite Valley.

Tuolumne Meadows, the only developed area, has a visitor center, store, cafe, mountaineering shop, campground, lodge, and gas station.

A free shuttle bus runs between Tuolumne Lodge and Olmsted Point every hour. The Tuolumne Meadows Hikers' Bus leaves Yosemite Valley and stops at Crane Flat and White Wolf on the way to Tuolumne Meadows Lodge every day. There is a charge, the amount depending upon where you want to be dropped off. A schedule and map of shuttle stops are available at the visitor center.

19 Dog Lake

A steady uphill climb takes you to the shore of this pretty little lake tucked in behind Lembert Dome.

Distance: 3.2 miles out and back
Elevation change: 600 feet
Approximate hiking time: 2 to 4 hours
Trail surface: Rocky packed earth
Difficulty: Moderate
Map: *USGS Tioga Pass*

Best time to go: Late spring to fall, whenever the Tioga Road is open
Facilities: Picnic tables and toilets at the trailhead but no potable water; supplies, telephone, and groceries available at the Tuolumne Meadows store, about 0.5 mile west on the Tioga Road

Finding the trailhead: From the west follow the Tioga Road (CA 120) eastward past the Tuolumne Meadows Visitor Center, store, and campground, all on the right (south) side of the road. About 150 yards beyond the bridge over the Tuolumne River, turn left (north) into the Lembert Dome parking area.

From the east (Tioga Pass) follow the Tioga Road past the turnoff to the Wilderness Center on the left (south). The sign for the center reads WILDERNESS PERMITS, PACIFIC CREST, JOHN MUIR. About 100 yards beyond the sign, turn right (north) into the Lembert Dome lot. GPS: N37 52.38' / W119 21.13'

The Hike

Set out northward from the Lembert Dome/Dog Lake trailhead sign through lodgepole pines. Cross an open rocky slab polished to a high sheen in places by glaciers and reenter the forest. At 0.2 mile a trail comes in from the stables to the left

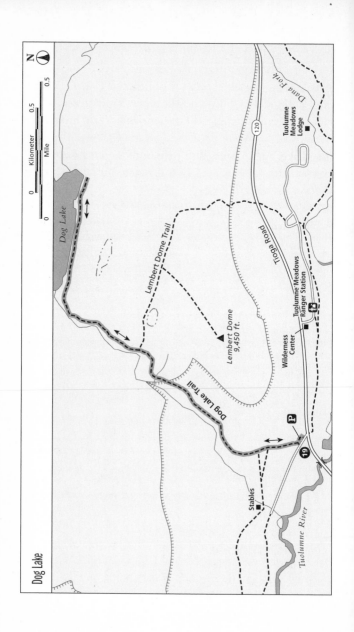

Dog Lake

(west). Take the right (north) fork. Just beyond, another trail comes in from the stables. Keep right (north) again. Climb steeply alongside the sheer face of Lembert Dome and then cross a little creek. The grade becomes less extreme.

At 1.1 miles a trail cuts off to the right (east) around the back of Lembert Dome. Continue straight (north) toward Dog Lake. At 1.5 miles turn right onto the Dog Lake Trail, and at 1.6 miles reach an opening in the forest that frames the lake perfectly. The sign at the lake says the water level is 9,240 feet, but it is marked 9,170 feet on the USGS topographic map. Take your pick.

Dog Lake is surrounded on three sides by lodgepole pines, but at the far east end a green (or golden, depending on the season) meadow provides the foreground for the huge red bulks of Mount Dana and Mount Gibbs.

Camping is not permitted here, tempting as it may be. The area is too delicate and too close to the busy road and would be trampled in no time. If you have decided not to walk all the way around the lake, return the way you came.

Miles and Directions

0.0 Trailhead.
0.1 Dog Lake/Lembert Dome split.
0.2 Trail to stables.
1.1 Pass trail to Lembert Dome on the right. Keep straight.
1.5 Dog Lake cutoff.
1.6 Reach Dog Lake. Retrace your steps.
3.2 Return to trailhead.

Option:

The official, mapped trail continues for about 0.5 mile along the south shore of the lake, but it is possible to circumambulate the lake, adding about 1.5 miles to your hike. There is no specific trail to follow. The meadow around the lakeshore, especially at the east and north ends, can be boggy and wet and is very fragile. Travel with care. At the northeast end of the lake, you will have a good view of Cathedral Peak poking up through the forest.

20 Lembert Dome

Lembert Dome—among the premiere features of Tuolumne Meadows—is the huge, lopsided, smoothly polished mound of granite just north of the Tioga Road. This loop will take you all the way around the dome, providing some great views along the way. There are even better views from the top, of course, but the route is strenuous and slippery and far beyond the definition of an "easy" hike. You can follow the route in either direction, but it will be described clockwise here.

Distance: 3.1-mile loop
Elevation change: 500 feet
Approximate hiking time: 2 to 3 hours
Trail surface: Packed forest floor, sometimes rocky
Difficulty: Moderate
Map: *USGS Tioga Pass*
Best time to go: Late June through mid-Sept, when the Tioga Road is open
Facilities: Picnic tables and toilets at the trailhead but no potable water; supplies, telephone, and groceries available at the Tuolumne Meadows store, about 0.5 mile west on the Tioga Road

Finding the trailhead: From the west follow the Tioga Road (CA 120) past the Tuolumne Meadows Visitor Center, store, cafe, and campground, all on the right (south) side of the road. About 150 yards beyond the bridge over the Tuolumne River, turn left (north) into the Lembert Dome parking area.

From the east (Tioga Pass) follow the Tioga Road past the turnoff to the Wilderness Center on the left (south) side of the road. Continue for about 100 yards and turn right (north) into the Lembert Dome parking area. GPS: N37 52.38' / W119 21.13'

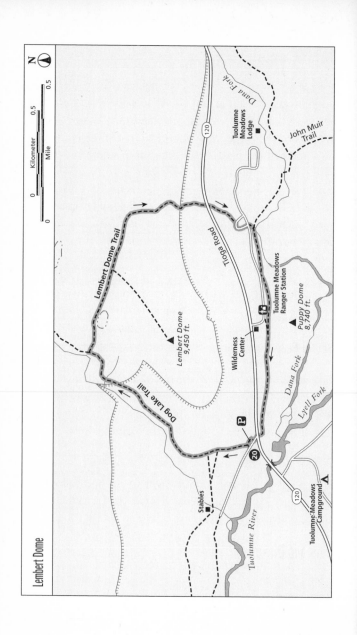

Lembert Dome

N

0   Kilometer   0.5

0   Mile   0.5

Dana Fork

Tuolumne Meadows Lodge

John Muir Trail

120

Tioga Road

Lembert Dome Trail

Lembert Dome 9,450 ft.

Tuolumne Meadows Ranger Station

Puppy Dome 8,740 ft.

Wilderness Center

Dog Lake Trail

P

Dana Fork

Lyell Fork

20

Stables

Tuolumne River

Tuolumne Meadows Campground

120

The Hike

Set out northward from the trailhead, past the picnic tables and restrooms from the Lembert Dome/Dog Lake trailhead sign. Pass beneath lodgepole pines and then cross an open, rocky slab where the route is marked by big boulders. Glaciers polished the granite to a high sheen in patches. If you look carefully you can see striations or scratches in the rock that show the direction in which the rivers of ice flowed.

At 0.2 mile a trail comes in from the stables to the left (west). Take the right (north) fork. Just beyond, another trail comes in from the same direction. Keep right (north) again.

Climb alongside the sheer face of Lembert Dome, then cross a little creek. The grade becomes more gradual. At 1.1 miles turn right (east) at the signed junction. The left fork goes north and uphill to Dog Lake. Saunter along an almost flat path, passing a little pond at the base of the dome.

At 1.7 miles reach another junction, not shown on the topo map; this one leads to the top of Lembert Dome. Your trail continues downhill to the left (south). Follow the steep switchbacks downhill to the Tioga Road. Cross the road at 2.5 miles; continue 0.1 mile to the parking lot on a small side road that leads to Tuolumne Meadows Lodge. Cross the road to the south and find a trail sign marking the John Muir Trail at 2.6 miles. Turn right (west) and follow the John Muir Trail alongside the Tioga Road to where you can cross the road at the Lembert Dome parking area.

Miles and Directions

0.0 Trailhead.

0.2 Pass the trails from the stables.

1.3 Reach the Lembert Dome/Dog Lake trail junction.

1.7 Pass the trail to the top of the dome.

2.5 Cross the Tioga Road.

2.6 Turn right (west) at the sign onto the John Muir Trail.

3.1 Return to the trailhead.

21 Pothole Dome

Pothole Dome looks like a much smaller version of Lembert Dome at the other end of Tuolumne Meadows. Interesting glacial features and great views make it such a popular hike that the vegetation between the road and the dome is in danger of becoming trampled. Please stay on the trail.

Distance: 1.0 mile out and back
Elevation change: 200 feet
Approximate hiking time: 30 minutes to 1 hour
Trail surface: Grassy meadow and slickrock

Difficulty: Easy
Map: *USGS Falls Ridge*
Best time to go: All summer, whenever the Tioga Road is open
Facilities: None at the trailhead

Finding the trailhead: Following the Tioga Road (CA 120), drive or ride the Tuolumne Meadows shuttle about 1.5 miles west of the visitor center. The parking area and trailhead are on the right (north) side of the road. There are several signs, including an interpretive panel about life in the meadow. GPS: N37 52.38' / W119 21.13'

The Hike

The trail skirts the meadow to the west and crosses over to the dome along the edge of the forest. It then swings right (east), back toward the low end of the dome, describing a wide U. Skirt the edge of the dome until you reach a convenient place to start up the long, smooth slope to its summit.

Here you will find a number of fine examples of glacial activity. There are patches of glacial polish, rock surfaces buffed to an almost blinding sheen by the movement of fine

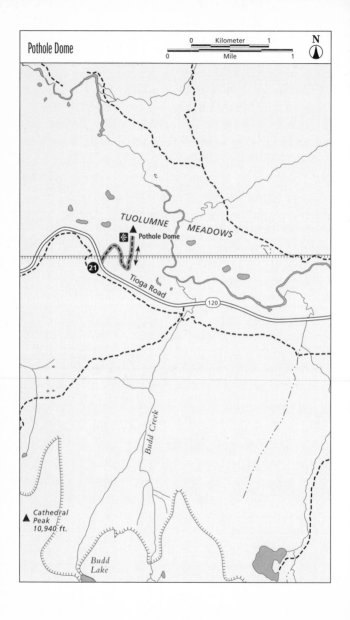

Pothole Dome

TUOLUMNE MEADOWS

Pothole Dome

Tioga Road

120

21

Budd Creek

Cathedral
Peak
10,940 ft.

Budd
Lake

0 ___ Kilometer ___ 1
0 ___ Mile ___ 1

grit dragged across the rock by moving ice. Huge boulders improbably perched on top of the dome were deposited there by the glaciers. Here and there are the potholes for which the dome was named, hollowed out by swirling water trapped beneath the glacial ice.

Enjoy the spectacular 360-degree view from the top, which includes the northern boundary country of the park; Mount Gibbs, Mount Dana, and Lembert Dome to the east; and the Cathedral Range to the south. Return, slowly and carefully, to the trailhead using the same trail.

Miles and Directions

0.0 Trailhead.

0.5 Reach the summit of Pothole Dome. Carefully retrace your steps.

1.0 Return to the trailhead.

22 Soda Springs and Parsons Lodge

A wide, sandy trail heads right into the heart of enormous Tuolumne Meadows amid a riot of wildflowers and crosses the Tuolumne River as it winds its sinuous way through the meadow. Beyond, you can visit mysterious Soda Springs and stop at historic Parsons Lodge, which houses exhibits of early days in Yosemite.

Distance: 1.2 miles out and back

Elevation change: 40 feet

Approximate hiking time: 1 to 2 hours

Trail surface: Packed earth and gravel road

Difficulty: Easy

Maps: *USGS Tioga Pass* and *Vogelsang Peak*

Best time to go: All summer, whenever the Tioga Road is open

Facilities: Food, water, gas, post office, and telephone available nearby in Tuolumne Meadows village

Finding the trailhead: From the visitor center in Tuolumne Meadows, drive about 150 yards east on the Tioga Road (CA 120) to the signed trailhead on the left (north) side of the road. GPS: N37 52.20' / W119 22.13'

The Hike

The trail begins amid an expanse of wildflowers such as purple meadow penstemon and shooting stars, white pussytoes, and yellow goldenrod. The Tuolumne River lies ahead, and off to the right (east) is long, sloping Lembert Dome. Farther beyond, rise the two red bulks of Mounts Dana and Gibbs. To their right is gray-granite Mammoth Peak.

At the main channel of the river, the path crosses a wood and stone footbridge. Pause here and turn around for

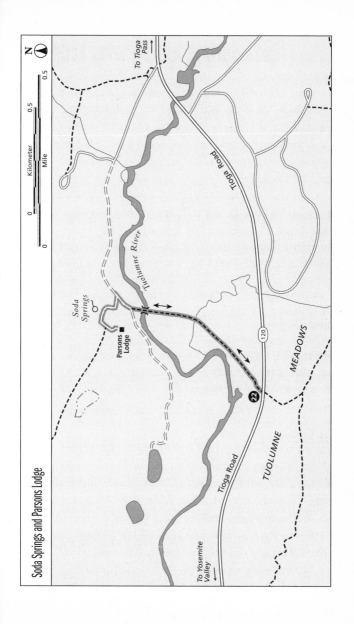

Soda Springs and Parsons Lodge

a panoramic view of the Cathedral Range to the south. The spires of Cathedral Peak itself, Echo Peak, and the Cockscomb rise behind smoothly rounded Fairview Dome.

Just beyond the bridge, the trail intersects a gravel road at 0.4 mile. Turn left (west) here; proceed about 50 yards to another sign directing you right (north) and up a little slope to Soda Springs and Parsons Lodge (0.6 mile).

Parsons Lodge, built of local stone by the Sierra Club in 1915 and sold to the National Park Service in 1973, is open daily during summer and contains exhibits on the history of the area. Next door, the log-built McCauley Cabin houses Park Service volunteers, who are eager to share information about the area. Rest for a while on the rocks in front of the lodge to watch the activities of the marmot families who live in burrows nearby.

From the lodge head toward the tumbledown, roofless log structure clearly visible to the east. Here naturally carbonated Soda Springs bubbles out of the ground in dozens of places, staining the soil red-brown. It's a good place to see mule deer, which come to lick the minerals deposited by the springs. You can spend a whole day wandering these meadows, using the well-marked trails to create your own loop, or you can return the way you came to the Tioga Road.

Miles and Directions

0.0 Trailhead.

0.4 Reach the gravel road.

0.6 Arrive at Parsons Lodge. Retrace your steps. (**Option:** Create a loop with additional meadows trails.)

1.2 Return to the trailhead.

23 Lyell Fork

This route is part of the famous John Muir Trail and the Pacific Crest Trail. It follows the Tuolumne River to a set of bridges at the foot of a grand meadow, one of the prettiest places in the park. You will probably want to spend hours there, so allow plenty of time.

Distance: 1.2 miles out and back
Elevation change: 60 feet
Approximate hiking time: 30 minutes to 1 hour
Trail surface: Rocky packed earth through forest
Difficulty: Easy

Maps: USGS *Tioga Pass* and *Vogelsang Peak*
Best time to go: All summer, whenever the Tioga Road is open
Facilities: None at the trailhead; food, phones, gas, water, and restrooms available less than 1 mile west on the Tioga Road

Finding the trailhead: From the west follow the Tioga Road (CA 120) eastward past the Tuolumne Meadows Visitor Center, store, and campground, all on the right (south) side of the road. Cross the bridge over the Tuolumne River. About 0.5 mile beyond the bridge, turn right (south) at the entrance to the Wilderness Center and follow the road as it curves left (east) for 0.5-mile to the Dog Lake parking lot on the left (north). Store any food or ice chests in the bear-proof boxes provided. Do not leave anything that looks or smells like food in your car. This parking lot fills up quickly; the earlier you arrive, the better your chances of finding a parking space. GPS: N37 52.33' / W119 20.07'

The Hike

Cross the road south of the parking lot to the trailhead sign. The trail rambles alongside the Dana Fork of the Tuolumne

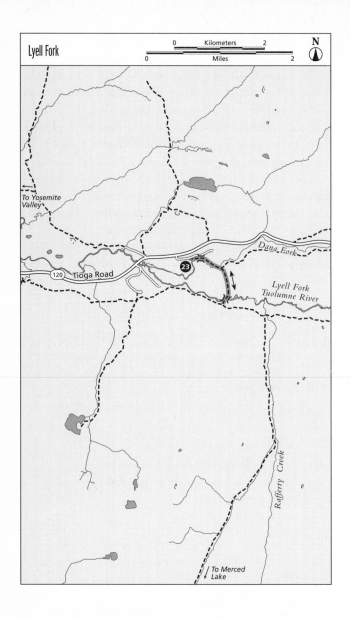

Kilometers

Miles

N

To Yosemite
Valley

Dana Fork

120 Tioga Road

23

Lyell Fork
Tuolumne River

Rafferty Creek

To Merced
Lake

River before crossing it on a footbridge at 0.2 mile. Ignore the sign that points north to the Tuolumne Meadows Lodge. Instead turn left (east) just after the crossing. The trail continues along the Dana Fork before swinging south to the junction with the Gaylor Lakes Trail at 0.3 mile. Keep right (south), then pass a marshy area on the left (east). Cross a low rocky rise and turn right (south) to reach the two bridges over the Lyell Fork of the Tuolumne River.

The scene from the bridges must be one of the most sublime in Yosemite. The river is a brilliant turquoise ribbon winding through the long, green meadow. The massive gray hulk on the left (southeast) is Mammoth Peak (not to be confused with Mammoth Mountain, the ski resort, which lies farther south). Where the river reaches the bridges, it rushes over smoothly rounded rocks, swirling in beautiful patterns that have hollowed out perfectly round shallow bowls in the granite before tumbling into clear pools.

When you can tear yourself away, retrace your steps to the trailhead.

Miles and Directions

0.0 Dog Lake trailhead.

0.2 Cross the bridge over Dana Fork and pass the junction with the Tuolumne Meadows Lodge Trail.

0.3 Reach the junction with the Gaylor Lakes Trail.

0.6 Arrive at the twin bridges over the Lyell Fork.

1.2 Return to the trailhead.

Hetch Hetchy

Hetch Hetchy Reservoir, completed in 1923 and expanded in 1938, provides water and power for the city of San Francisco. Before the O'Shaughnessy Dam captured and tamed the Tuolumne River, the Hetch Hetchy Valley was said to rival Yosemite in scenic beauty. John Muir's famous, if fruitless, battle against the dam brought the need to preserve such wilderness treasures to the attention of the American public and gave impetus to the growth of the National Park Service and to the conservation movement as a whole. Today a campaign is under way to convince legislators to raze the dam, drain the reservoir, and allow Hetch Hetchy to return to its natural state.

The area around the lake has the best display of springtime wildflowers in the park. It's a great place to hike in early season, when the higher country is still under snow, and it's pleasant in October when the black oaks change color. In midsummer it's dry and hot. No swimming or boating is allowed in the reservoir.

To reach the main Hetch Hetchy trailhead at O'Shaughnessy Dam, you must leave Yosemite park at the Big Oak Flat entrance station (if you are coming from the east) and reenter the park at the Hetch Hetchy entrance station, about 8 miles up Evergreen Road. From the west, turn off the highway before you reach the main (Big Oak

Flat) entrance station. Ask about the condition of the road before you start out—it washes out regularly and may be closed for repairs.

Note: Because the reservoir is a crucial source of water and power for San Francisco, park rangers at the entrance kiosk record license numbers of all vehicles entering and leaving the area.

24 Wapama Falls

The area around the Hetch Hetchy Reservoir has the best springtime wildflower display in the park, and it's a good place for a hike when the higher country is still under snow. In springtime, snowmelt water pours over Wapama Falls with tremendous force. By midsummer the falls are dry and the hike can be uncomfortably hot, but in October, when the leaves of the black oaks turn bright yellow and the temperature cools, the trip to this out-of-the-way spot is worth the drive.

Distance: 5.0 miles out and back
Elevation change: 200 feet
Approximate hiking time: 3 to 5 hours
Trail surface: Abandoned road, rocky trail
Difficulty: More challenging
Map: *USGS Lake Eleanor*

Best time to go: Mid-Apr to June (hot and dry later in summer); Oct for foliage
Facilities: Water, restrooms, and phone on the right side of the road just before the dam and parking area on the one-way loop road

Finding the trailhead: Drive 1 mile west of the Big Oak Flat entrance station to Yosemite National Park on CA 120. Turn right (north) onto Evergreen Road and drive about 7 miles. At Camp Mather turn right (northeast) on Hetch Hetchy Road. After about 1 mile, pass through the park entrance station, where you will be given a day-use permit for your dashboard and your vehicle license number will be registered. These precautions have been in effect since the 9/11 terrorist attacks, since Hetch Hetchy Reservoir contains the water supply for the city of San Francisco. Continue for 8 miles to where the road ends in a one-way loop. The parking area is partway around the dam and just beyond it. GPS: N37 56.19' / W119 47.15'

The Hike

Hetch Hetchy Reservoir—built between 1914 and 1923 and expanded in 1938—provides water and power for the City of San Francisco, so no swimming or boating is allowed.

To begin the hike, walk across the dam past some historical markers and colorful interpretive panels about the benefits of the dam installed by the City of San Francisco. On the far side, at 0.1 mile, enjoy the troupe of acrobatic swallows swooping and diving before the entrance to a dark and dripping tunnel. Pass through the tunnel and continue along the level road skirting the lake.

The roadside is lined with live oak, bay trees, and poison oak, along with dozens of species of wildflowers. The low elevation here makes this a likely spot for encounters with snakes of several kinds, including rattlers. They are not aggressive, but they should be avoided. If you're lucky you'll catch the spring migration of millions of little brown-and-orange California newts. In the sunny places by the trail grow beautiful pink-and-yellow harlequin lupines. Water trickles down cracks in the rock to nourish buttercups, monkeyflowers, columbines, and many other species.

The road climbs slowly for a while, then at 0.9 mile the trail to the falls leaves the road and turns right (east). The left (north) route leads to Lake Vernon. The Wapama Falls Trail rises and falls and curves back and forth past more delicate little gardens, waterfalls, and pools. Kolana Rock broods darkly over the reservoir on the other side.

Tueeulala Fall tumbles down over the trail. Early in the season you'll probably get your feet wet as you pass, but by June the little waterfall is usually dry. The trail continues

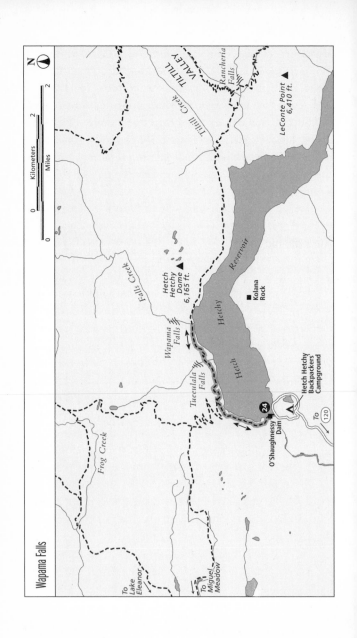

along the cliff above the lake, climbing and descending for 1.5 miles more until the spray and thunder of Wapama Falls make themselves felt. Toward the bottom, the falls split into several sections, each of which is crossed on a separate footbridge. Sometimes the bridges are underwater shin-deep, although safe to wade; at other times the force of the torrent is so great that it is not safe to cross. You can enjoy the falls from either side or from the middle—if you crave a refreshing shower.

Return the way you came.

Miles and Directions

0.0 Hetch Hetchy trailhead.
0.1 Pass through the tunnel.
0.9 Reach the Lake Vernon Trail junction.
2.5 Arrive at Wapama Falls. Retrace your steps.
5.0 Return to the trailhead.

About the Author

Suzanne Swedo, director of W.I.L.D. (www.wildswedo .com), has backpacked the mountains of every continent. She has led groups into the wilderness for more than twenty-five years and teaches wilderness survival and natural sciences for individuals, schools, universities, museums, and organizations such as the Yosemite Association and the Sierra Club. She is author of *Wilderness Survival, Hiking Yosemite National Park, Hiking California's Golden Trout Wilderness,* and *Adventure Travel Tips* for FalconGuides. She lectures and consults about backpacking, botany, and survival on radio and television, as well as in print.